For Richard

© Copyright text Mathew Price 1990

© Copyright illustration Atsuko Morozumi 1990

Designed by Herman Lelie

Produced by Mathew Price Ltd

Printed in Hong Kong

First published in 1990 by The Bodley Head Children's Books,
an imprint of the Random Century Group Ltd.
20 Vauxhall Bridge Road, London, SW1V 2SA

Random Century South Africa (Pty) Ltd
PO Box 337, Bergvlei, 2012 South Africa

A CIP catalogue record for this book
is available from The British Library

ISBN 0-370-31476 X

AND ONE GORILLA

A Counting Book

Atsuko Morozumi

THE BODLEY HEAD
LONDON

Here is a list of things I love.
One gorilla.

Two butterflies among the flowers
and one gorilla.

Three budgerigars in my house
and one gorilla.

Four squirrels in the woods
and one gorilla.

Five pandas in the snow
and one gorilla.

Six rabbits in a field
and one gorilla.

Seven frogs by the fence
and one gorilla.

Eight fish in the sea
and one gorilla.

Nine birds among the leaves
and one gorilla.

Ten cats in my garden
and one gorilla.

10 cats

9 birds

8 fish

7 frogs

6 rabbits

5 pandas

4 squirrels

3 budgerigars

2 butterflies

But where is my gorilla?

Ah, there he is.